IMAGES
of Sport

CREWE ALEXANDRA
FOOTBALL CLUB

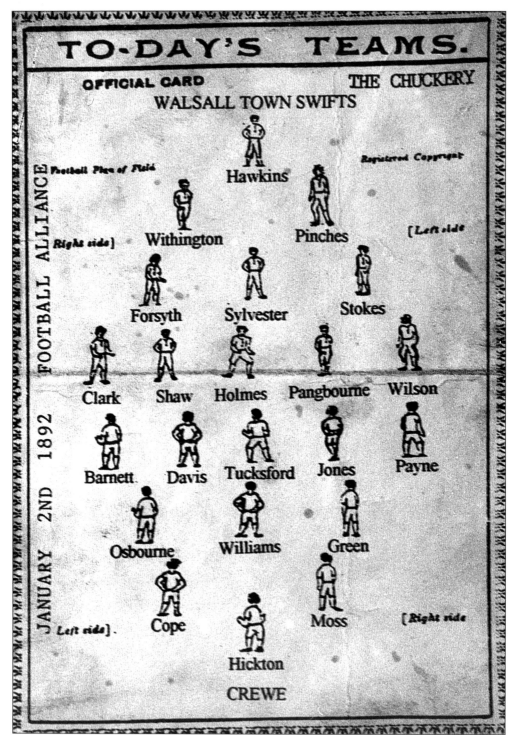

A football card for an Alliance fixture between Walsall Swifts and Crewe Alexandra on 2 January 1892 at The Chuckery. Crewe lost the game 3-1, with Jones scoring the lone Crewe goal. This is the earliest example of a 'programme' involving Crewe seen to date.

IMAGES
of Sport

CREWE ALEXANDRA
FOOTBALL CLUB

Compiled by
Harold Finch

TEMPUS

First published 1999
Reprinted 2000, 2001
Copyright © Harold Finch, 1999

Tempus Publishing Limited
The Mill, Brimscombe Port,
Stroud, Gloucestershire, GL5 2QG

ISBN 0 7524 1545 X

Typesetting and origination by
Tempus Publishing Limited
Printed in Great Britain by
Midway Clark Printing, Wiltshire

Present and forthcoming sports titles from Tempus:

Anfield Voices
Bristol Rovers FC
Bury FC
Cardiff City FC
Charlton FC
Crystal Palace FC
Exeter City FC
Oxford United FC
Plymouth Argyle FC
Reading FC
Roker Park Voices
Sheffield United FC
Stoke City FC
Sunderland FC
Swansea Town FC
Tranmere Rovers FC

Glamorgan CCC
The Scarborough Festival
Somerset CCC
Yorkshire CCC

Please contact Tempus Publishing (01453 883300) for a full catalogue.

Contents

Foreword

Players and managers come and go at all clubs and these days the owners change frequently. The fans though, nearly always support the same team all their life. All the clubs I have worked at have some supporters who have been following their favourite team for decades. However, even amongst these extraordinary men, Harold Finch's devotion to Crewe Alexandra stands out as being quite exceptional. Seventy-two years of age, he has been supporting the Alex for sixty-five years, been editing or involved with the programme for fifty years and is still going strong. All that has not been enough for him, and during much of that time he has been a meticulous collector of photographs, programmes and other memorabilia relating to the club. He is both official and unofficial historian of Crewe Alexandra and his collection covers items from before the turn of the century to the present day.

I have only been here for the past sixteen years and Harold often produces something from his collection when we travel to away games on the coach. Many of these photographs are accompanied by a story which will I am sure make this publication fascinating for all Alex fans, young or not so young. For all of us it will bring back rich memories. Harold, I know, is proud that we will be able to share in his obsession with the fortunes of Crewe Alexandra.

Dario Gradi MBE

Introduction

Although born in Burton-on-Trent, apart from a four-year spell, I have lived all my life in Crewe. At the age of seven, I was taken by my uncle, the late J.P. Brown, to Gresty Road to see Crewe play Accrington Stanley. The date was Saturday 10 March 1934 and Crewe won 4-2.

From that date onwards, there has only been one club for me – Crewe Alexandra. Unlike many clubs, when they hit the headlines it would not be because of a promotion campaign, for that was an element that did not figure in their early history. Finally, in 1963, promotion became a possibility, with the outcome depending on the final game of the season, a home fixture with Exeter City. A Frank Lord goal ensured the Alex's triumph and at long last supporters were able to show their relief and joy.

There have been other promotions but so far the club have not yet won a divisional championship. Third or fourth place finishes and a play-off final victory have been the club's route to playing a higher grade of football so far.

Throughout the club's long history, there has always been a nucleus of dedicated supporters. Whilst in the past these numbers may have sometimes dwindled, the tide has turned in recent years and the numbers who now attend on a regular basis give the club something to build on.

In the difficult years – and there have been quite a number during my long association with the club – my interest has never waned. I have been delighted to find, through my contacts in the wider world of football, that Crewe Alexandra has become a club to admire, for the way it is managed, both on and off the field, and for their style of play.

It is extremely difficult to pick out individual games, performances or players that will find universal agreement with supporters, but older fans will recall two half-back lines that were much admired for a long time. The first was Meaney, Lees and Murphy to be followed by Stott, Barnes and Gannon. Then there were such stalwarts as Peter Leigh and Tommy Lowry, ball players like Frank Mitcheson, Stan Bowles and Gordon Wallace, not to mention the home-grown talents of Johnny King and Frank Blunstone.

There have been numerous post-war managers, including Jimmy McGuigan, Ernie Tagg, Harry Gregg and Tony Waddington. It was in the 1960s that Ernie Tagg brought fans back to Gresty Road with his attacking style of play, whilst in the 1980s stability became the order of the day – and still continues.

When Dario Gradi arrived in the summer of 1983, people in the area knew little about him.

What a change there has been since. He is the longest surviving manager in the Football League and many of the young players given their chance of League football under him have gone on to higher things. Training facilities are now second to none and, in the years to come, many more young players will become just as familiar as those nurtured during his early days.

My own personal involvement now spans almost half a century and I have known both the managers and the playing staff for long periods of time. I have indeed been fortunate to work with and live alongside so many people from Crewe Alexandra FC. For over four decades I edited the Crewe Alexandra matchday programme and before that I had served on the Executive Committee of the Supporters Association and was the founder of the original section of the Junior Supporters Club.

The club marked my work with them when they appointed me an Honorary Life Vice President in 1984. This has given me a great deal of pride and I have been fortunate to travel with the team on journeys taking in the length and breadth of the country.

Like many supporters, I had always wanted to see Crewe Alexandra appearing at Wembley – this I have now done on two occasions. The first did not have a successful outcome but the second, in 1997, did, the memories of that day, right from early morning to the time that the team arrived back in Crewe will live with me forever.

Season 1999/2000 will mark the time that Gresty Road, home of Crewe Alexandra FC becomes an all-seater stadium with a capacity of 10,000. Names such as the Railway End, Gresty Road End, Popular Side and Paddock may not be used in official circles, but long standing supporters will continue to refer to them and they, like the name of the club, will survive.

Harold Finch.

Harold Finch

Acknowledgements

I would like to place on record my thanks to those who have helped with the loan of their photographs and scrapbooks, thus supplementing my own archives. These people are: Eric Barnes, Frank Blunstone, David Bowyer, Keith Clayton, Arthur Davies, Dario, Mrs J. Dyer, Chris Jones, Colin McLean, Mrs Jack Meaney, Roy Greer (a valuable friend for many years), Brian Hassall, Alan Newton, Peter Robinson, Robert Sproston, Sentinel Newspapers, Dave Slack, Ernie Tagg and John Tibbetts. After a long search, Ernie Tagg found his scrapbooks and added to the final choice right at the last minute.

Last, but not least, I would like to thank my son Stephen, for both his work behind the camera and for his advice on the technical side, and my wife, who, through the final stages of selection, showed infinite patience.

I feel confident that a great many memories will be revived through this book and faces will be put to names that have been familiar in conversations in many households. However, space as always is a limiting factor, and my aim has been to spread the information as evenly as possible throughout the club's long history – time will tell whether this has been achieved.

One
The Early Years
1877-1919

Founded in 1877 as an adjunct of the Crewe Alexandra Cricket Club, the team played friendly games initially, entering the Football Alliance in the 1889/90 season and Division Two in 1892/93. These players featured are from a group pictured in around 1886/87.

FOOTBALL!

Grand Match.

CHESHIRE CUP COMPETITION!

SEMI-FINAL TIE.

CHESTER COLLEGE

v.

CREWE Alexandra!

AT

VICTORIA ROAD, ON SATURDAY NEXT,

MARCH 22ND.

KICK OFF AT 3 O'CLOCK PROMPT.

ADMISSION, 3d.; Reserved Ground, 6d.; Ladies & Subscribers Free

PROBABLE PLAYERS:

CHESTER COLLEGE:		CREWE ALEXANDRA:	
BAGOT, Goal.		PARKER, Goal	
SHERRATT,	} Backs.	W. DOWNES,	} Backs.
JONES.		G. WYTCHERLEY,	
SMITH,		POWELL,	
WHITE, *Capt.*	} Half Backs.	COOKSON,	} Half Backs
CLAYTON,		BENHAM,	
Forwards:		Forwards:	
STRINGER,	} Left Wing.	TAYLOR,	} Left Wing
BRISCOE,		SNELSON,	
BENTLEY, Centre.		GARNER, Centre	
COULSON,	} Right Wing	HOUGHTON,	} Right Wing
PIXTON,		WATKINS,	

W. COLLINS, PRINTER AND BOOKBINDER, PARK GREEN, MACCLESFIELD.

A single sheet issue for the Cheshire Senior Cup semi-final tie at Macclesfield on Saturday 22 March 1884. Crewe equalised in the final minute to secure a replay, which they won 2-0.

Cheshire Senior Cup winners' medals won by H. Bayman of Crewe Alexandra in consecutive seasons (1887 and 1888). The victory in 1888, 9-0 against Chester, is still a record score in this competition.

GRAND FOOTBALL MATCH

At MIDDLEWICH,

On SATURDAY, JANUARY 9th. 1886, at 2-30.

THIRD ROUND WELSH CUP.

NORTHWICH

VICTORIA

versus

Crewe Alexandra.

PROBABLE PLAYERS :--

ALEXANDRA (Red & White)	VICTORIA (Red & Black)
C. Cross	E. Harper
F. J. Marsh W. Downes	F. W. Hughes E. Molyneux
G. Wytcherley W. S. Bell	W. H. Hughes J. Maddock
F. Halfpenny (Captain)	J. Rose
A. Payne J. Pearson	J. Malam E. Turnbull
T. H. Cross E. Payne T. Snelson	T. Hankey E. R Denton (Capt.) T. Lever
Umpire, Mr. T. M. Abraham.	Umpire, Mr. F. R. Hobson.

Referee—Mr. T. ORMEROD, Accrington.

Admission 4d.

A SPECIAL TRAIN will leave Crewe at 1 p.m.   Tickets
can be obtained at the Station not later than 12-50.
Return Fare, ONE SHILLING.

Henry Taylor, "Caxton" Printing Offices, High Street, Crewe.

Match details of a third round tie in the Welsh Cup at Northwich on Saturday 9 January 1886.
Printed in Crewe, this may have been used as a programme. The game finished as a 2-2 draw.

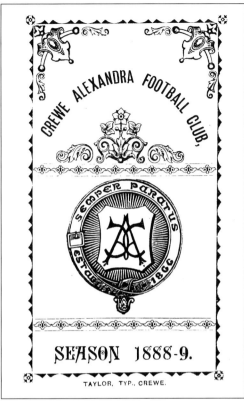
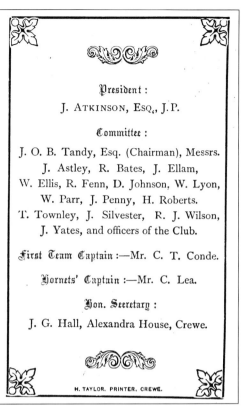

A season ticket from 1888/89, the first season in the Football Alliance. *Above*: The front and back covers. *Below*: The full fixture list for the campaign. The club ran three teams at this time. The reserve side, called 'The Hornets', played in black and yellow striped jerseys, befitting of their title.

The images above carry the following text:

Left cover: CREWE ALEXANDRA FOOTBALL CLUB. SEMPER PARATUS. Estab. 1866. SEASON 1888-9. TAYLOR, TYP., CREWE.

Right cover:

President :
J. Atkinson, Esq., J.P.

Committee :
J. O. B. Tandy, Esq. (Chairman), Messrs.
J. Astley, R. Bates, J. Ellam,
W. Ellis, R. Fenn, D. Johnson, W. Lyon,
W. Parr, J. Penny, H. Roberts.
T. Townley, J. Silvester, R. J. Wilson,
J. Yates, and officers of the Club.

First Team Captain :—Mr. C. T. Conde.

Hornets' Captain :—Mr. C. Lea.

Hon. Secretary :
J. G. Hall, Alexandra House, Crewe.

H. TAYLOR, PRINTER, CREWE.

FIRST TEAM
Holders of the Cheshire Challenge Cup 1887-8, 1888-9.

Date.	Club.	Grnd	Goals Alex	Opp
1888.				
Sept. 8	Bootle	Home		
,, 15	South Shore	Home		
,, 22	Walsall Town Swifts	Away		
,, 29	Derby Midland	Home		
Oct. 6	Mitchell St. George's	Away		
,, 13	Leek	Home		
,, 20	Port Vale	Home		
,, 27	Darwen	Away		
Nov. 3	Cheshire v. Derbyshire	Away		
,, 10	Mitchell St. George's	Home		
,, 17	Macclesfield	Away		
,, 24	1st. Round Cheshire Cup			
Dec. 1	Cam Unity v. Cheshire	Home		
,, 8	Leek	Home		
,, 15	Macclesfield	Home		
,, 22	Bootle	Away		
,, 25	Notts Rangers	Home		
,, 26	Davenham	Home		
,, 29	Port Vale	Away		
1889.				
Jan. 5	2nd Round Cheshire Cup			
,, 12	Derby Midland	Away		
,, 19	Walsall Town Swifts	Home		
,, 26	Chester	Away		
Feb. 2	First Round English Cup			
,, 9	Darwen	Home		
,, 16	2nd Round English Cup			
,, 23	Semi-Final Cheshire Cup			
Mar. 2	3rd Round English Cup			
,, 9	South Shore	Away		
,, 16	Semi Final English Cup			
,, 23	Final Tie Cheshire Cup			
,, 30	Chester			
Apl. 6	Notts Rangers	Away		
,, 13				
,, 19	Lincoln City	Away		
,, 20	Gainsboro Trinity	Away		
,, 22	Grimsby Town	Away		

HORNETS' TEAM.
Holders of the Cheshire Junior Challenge Cup, 1887-8.
Holders of the Crewe & District Challenge Cup, 1886-7, 1887-8, 1888-9

Date.	Club.	Grnd	Goals Alex	Opp
1888.				
Sept. 8	Hanley Town	Away		
,, 15	Hartford St. John's	Away		
,, 22	Saltney	Home		
,, 29	Over Wanderers	Away		
Oct. 6	Burslem Wycliffe	Home		
,, 13	Stafford Rangers	Away		
,, 20	Port Vale Rovers	Away		
,, 27	Witton Britannia	Home		
Nov. 3	Cheshire Jun. v. Staffshire	Away		
,, 10	[Jun.			
,, 17	Whitchurch Town	Home		
,, 24	Newcastle Swifts	Away		
Dec. 1	1st Round Cheshire Jun. Cup			
,, 8	Macclesfield Swifts	Home		
,, 15	Shrewsbury Town Reserve	Away		
,, 22	Second Round Jun. Cup			
,, 25				
,, 26	Whitchurch Town	Away		
,, 29	Port Vale Rovers	Home		
1889.				
Jan. 5	Saltney	Away		
,, 12	Hartford St. John's	Home		
,, 19	3rd. Rd. Cheshire Jun. Cup			
,, 26	Chester Reserve	Home		
Feb. 2	Macclesfield Swifts	Home		
,, 9	Witton Britannia	Away		
,, 16	Semi-Fnl.Cheshire Jun Cup			
,, 23	Stoke Swifts			
Mar. 2	Shrewsbury Town Reserve	Home		
,, 9	Stafford Rangers	Home		
,, 16	Newcastle Swifts	Home		
,, 23	Burslem Wycliffe	Away		
,, 30	Chester Reserve	Away		
Apl. 6	Saltney	Home		
,, 13	Over Wanderers	Home		
,, 19				
,, 20				
,, 22				

RANGERS' TEAM.

Date.	Club.	Grnd	Goals Alex	Opp
1888.				
Sept. 1	Excelsior (Crewe)	Home		
,, 8	Saltney	Away		
,, 15				
,, 22	Kidsgrove	Home		
,, 29	Sandbach	Away		
Oct. 6	Sandbach	Home		
,, 13	Rockwood Villa	Away		
,, 20	Wem White Star	Away		
,, 27	Winnington Park	Home		
Nov. 3	Rockwood Villa	Home		
,, 10	Middlewich	Away		
,, 17	Smallthorne St. Saviours	Home		
,, 24	Excelsior (Crewe)	Away		
Dec. 1	Burslem St. Paul's	Home		
,, 8	Heaton Norris	Away		
,, 15				
,, 22	Stockton Heath	Home		
,, 24	Winnington Park	Away		
,, 29	Manchester St. Mary's	Home		
1889.				
Jan. 5	Kidsgrove	Away		
,, 12	Chester Trinity Lever	Home		
,, 19	Stockton Heath	Away		
,, 26				
Feby. 2	Chester Trinity Lever	Away		
,, 9	Manchester St. Mary's	Away		
,, 16	Smallthorne St. Saviour's	Away		
,, 23	Wem White Star	Home		
March 2	Burslem St. Paul's	Away		
,, 9	Heaton Norris	Home		
,, 16	Crewe Swifts	Away		
,, 23				
,, 30	Crewe Swifts	Home		
Apl. 6				
,, 13				
,, 19				
,, 20	Saltney	Home		
,, 22				

FOOTBALL ASSOCIATION CUP.
FOURTH ROUND.

Crewe Alexandra v. Swifts.—Replayed at Derby, resulting in a win for Crewe Alexandra by two goals to one. The weather was dull, and the turf very greasy. Crewe kicked off, and the Swifts at once gained an unproductive corner. Pearson retaliated for Crewe, but shot over the bar. Once during the first half the game was delayed through Cotterill and Bambridge being hurt simultaneously. But no goals were obtained before half-time. On resuming, Ingram made a good attempt to score for the Swifts, but shot wide. Crewe then obtained a free kick, and Pearson kicked a neat goal; this was followed immediately afterwards by another good goal from Price. Soon after restarting Challen made a splendid run down the right wing, and centred to Bambridge, who scored. Teams: CREWE ALEXANDRA.—Hickton, goal; Conde and Bayman, backs; Osborne, Halfpenny, and Bell, half-backs; Payne and Pearson (right), Price (centre), Ellis and Tinsley (left), forwards. SWIFTS.—H. A. Swepstone, goal; A. O. Davies and A. W. Platt, backs; F. E. Saunders, Humphrey-Jones, and C. Holden White, half-backs; J. B. Challen and W. H. Garne (right), G. H. Cotterill (centre), F. M. Ingram and E. C. Bambridge (left), forwards. Umpires, R. J. Smith (Derby) and Stacey (Sheffield); referee, Major Marindin (R E., president Football Association).

An eye-witness informs us that the referee (Major Marindin) in the Swifts v. Crewe tie at Derby was principally occupied during the match in cautioning the Crewe men for foul play, and asking their names. One or two of them are, if rumour is correct, to be reported to the Association Council. Why did not the Major use his authority, and order them off the field?

After the match, one of the Crewe officials drew a two-foot rule from his pocket, and proudly said, "This has won the match." True sportsmanlike instincts cannot be subdued!

Had Crewe lost the match we hear that they had a protest ready on three distinct grounds, each of which would have been stronger than that which upset the result of the previous match.

"Virtue rewarded" is the motto which the Crewe Alexandra F.C. has adopted.

The misfortunes of the Swifts may prove a blessing to football if the lessons of their recent experience are taken to heart by the Council of the Football Association on the one hand, and by amateur clubs on the other. The latter may at least be expected to count the cost before entering for the Cup, and to give the sportsmen of Crewe a wide berth in future.

SATURDAY'S FOOTBALL.

ASSOCIATION MATCHES.

ENGLISH CUP.—Semi-finals.

Crewe Alexandra v. Preston North End.—This match was played at Everton in beautiful weather. The thaw overnight had been very pronounced, and on reaching the enclosure the ground was found to be very sloppy, small pools of water being conspicuous in several parts. Long before the time announced for the kick-off people began to stream into the ground, which was literally packed when operations commenced. The teams stepped into the field as follow:—

PRESTON NORTH END.—Mills Roberts, goal; Howarth and N J Ross, backs; Holmes, Russell, and Graham, half-backs; Gordon, Ross, Goodall, Dewhurst, and Drummond, forwards.

CREWE.—Hickton, goal; Bayman and Conde, backs; Cope, Halfpenny, and Bell, half-backs; Ellis, Tinsley, Pearson, Payne, and Price, forwards.

Referee, Mr W H Jope, Wednesbury.

Prior to the start Crewe Alexandra lodged a protest against the state of the ground. North End won the toss, and Crewe started the ball at seven minutes past 3. North End at once assumed the aggressive, and a dribble by Drummond was splendidly stopped by Conde, who returned to mid-field. A claim for "hands" gave North End a free kick near the goal, and after Conde had partially relieved, Drummond kicked over the bar. Crewe then had a look in, and obtained a corner, which, however, proved fruitless. North End again looked dangerous, and some capital passing between the forwards resulted in Ross, jun., scoring the first goal, thirteen minutes from the start, amidst cheers. North End after this pressed their opponents, and a couple of corners fell to them in quick succession. The ground was now in a fearful condition, and it was as much as the players could do to keep their feet. Eventually Ross centred nicely, and Goodall shot the second goal for North End with a lightning shot. Two minutes afterwards North End had a goal disallowed for off-side play. The Crewe men played anything but a strong defensive game, and North End kept up a continuous attack, with the result that Goodall scored two goals in quick succession. Russell scored the fifth goal, and then Graham shot over the bar. Pearson put in a smart piece of play for Crewe, and then Gordon executed a brilliant run on the right for North End. Half-time arrived shortly afterwards, the score standing—North End, five goals; Crewe, none. Commencing the second half North End soon started to press. Payne, however, was prominent with a good run, and North End conceded a corner, but nothing came of it. After this Preston had matters pretty much their own way. Numerous shots were sent into the Crewe goal, but Hickton defended well, while North End missed one or two easy chances of scoring. A capital run by the Crewe right gave them a chance, Mills-Roberts handling the ball for the first time during the game. The play was much more even after this, but the final result was—

NORTH END .... 5 GOALS
CREWE ALEXANDRA .... NONE

The 1887/88 season was an exciting one for the club, involving the infamous 'two foot rule' incident. Crewe's FA Cup home tie with Swifts ended in a 2-2 draw and the match was replayed at Queens Ground, West Kensington on 17 December 1887. Before the match, Crewe officials noted that the crossbar at one end of the ground did not appear to be correct and used a two foot rule to confirm their suspicions. It was only after they had lost the game that a protest was made, an appeal upheld and a further replay ordered – which is described in one of the above articles. Comments from the *Pastime* magazine (left) show that the club was not too popular in football circles. The club did go on to reach the semi-final stage of the competition and the report of that game from the *Sporting Chronicle* of 20 February 1887 is shown above (right).

CREWE ALEXANDRA FOOTBALL CLUB.

PROGRAMME.

LONDON TOUR, XMAS, 1890.

Friday, Dec. 26th.

TEAM LEAVE CREWE STATION 3.30 A.M.
ARRIVE EUSTON 7.20 A.M. | BREAKFAST AT EDWARDS' HOTEL, EUSTON SQ. 8.0.
LEAVE VICTORIA 11.10 A.M. ARRIVE CHATHAM 12.10 P.M.
LUNCHEON AT CHATHAM 12.30.
———— MATCH, *versus* CHATHAM, at 2.30. ————
LEAVE CHATHAM FOR LONDON, 5.0 P.M. ARRIVE VICTORIA 6.20 P.M.
TEA AT RESTAURANT 6.45.
TEAM TO BE AT EDWARDS' HOTEL, AT 12.0, FOR BED.

Saturday, Dec. 27th.

BREAKFAST AT 9 O'CLOCK. LUNCHEON AT 12 O'CLOCK.
LEAVE EUSTON 12.40. ARRIVE WATFORD 1.25.
———— MATCH, *versus* 93rd HIGHLANDERS, at 2.15. ————
LEAVE WATFORD 4.30. ARRIVE WILLESDEN 4.38.
LEAVE WILLESDEN 5.42. ARRIVE CREWE 9.0.

J. G. HALL, Hon. Sec.

A souvenir card for the club's London tour, undertaken at Christmas 1890. Note the departure from Crewe at 3.30 am. The results on the tour were as follows: Chatham 2 Crewe Alexandra 3 (Bould, Pearson, own goal), 93rd Highlanders 0 Crewe Alexandra 2 (Bould, unspecified).

Two Alliance fixtures and a 'friendly' game at Doncaster made up this tour in Easter 1891, with the games providing plenty of goals. The results on the tour were: Ardwick 6 Crewe Alexandra 5, Grimsby 3 Crewe Alexandra 3, Doncaster Rovers 2 Crewe Alexandra 1. Ardwick later became Manchester City FC.

Crewe ⁖ Alexandra ⁖ Football ⁖ Club.

PROGRAMME.

EASTER TOUR, 1891.

FRIDAY, MARCH 27th.

Team leave Crewe Station 9.10 a.m. Arrive Manchester 10.0 a.m.
Brake to Ardwick meets Train.
MATCH versus ARDWICK at 11 o'clock.
Brake Ardwick to Manchester 1 o'clock.
Dinner at 2.0 p.m.
Leave Manchester 5.0 p.m. Arrive Cleethorpes 8.45 p.m.
Dinner at Cliff Hotel, 9.0 p.m.

SATURDAY, MARCH 28th.

Breakfast 9.0 a.m. Luncheon 12 o'clock.
ALLIANCE MATCH versus GRIMSBY TOWN 3.0 p.m.
Dinner at Cliff Hotel 6.0 p.m.
Leave Cliff Hotel for Grimsby Theatre 7.0 p.m.

SUNDAY, MARCH 29th.

Breakfast 9.0 a.m. Dinner 1.0 p.m. Tea 5.30 p.m.

MONDAY, MARCH 30th.

Breakfast Cliff Hotel 8.0 a.m. Leave Cleethorpes 9.0 a.m.
Luncheon at Doncaster 12 o'clock.
MATCH versus DONCASTER ROVERS 3.15 p.m.
Tea at Doncaster 5.30 p.m.
Leave Doncaster 6.25 p.m. Arrive Manchester 8.35 p.m.
Leave Manchester 9.15 ,, Arrive Crewe 10.28 ,,

WILMOT EARDLEY, PRINTER, CREWE.

Alexandra Park, Gresty Rd. Crewe

Grand Football Match

Arthur Brookfield's Benefit

By kind permission of the Directors of the Crewe
Alexandra Football Club and the Football Association.

On Wednesday, Sep. 12th, 1900
Kick-off 6 p.m.
STOKE (Full League) Team
VERSUS
Crewe Alexandra.

Tickets 4d. each.   Stand 3d. extra.

H. Taylor, Printer, Crewe.

An illustrated ticket for a benefit game granted to Arthur Brookfield, the club's popular outside right, on Wednesday 12 September 1900. The game finished Crewe 2 Stoke City 0.

Crewe's first game in the Birmingham League was on 7 September 1901, when they beat Coventry City 4-0. The players shown in the picture are, from left to right, back row: Coventry (goalkeeper). Second row: Lyons and Roberts (full-backs), Callows, Hall and Large (half-backs). Front row: Robertson, Hesham, Jones, Edgley, Kynnersley (forwards).

Above: A group photograph of the 1904/05 team, which had been sent by Birchenough, the goalkeeper, to a friend in South Africa. The players are wearing an unfamiliar white strip. *Below left*: Harry Clark was considered to be one of the best wing halves at Crewe during the club's Birmingham League days. A long-serving player, he was widely respected by the Crewe management and supporters. *Below right*: The front of the Keys Cup medal awarded to Harry at the end of the 1905/06 season. The Keys Cup was awarded to the highest finishing non-reserve side.

Team group for 1908/09, taken at the Gresty Road end of the ground. It is interesting to note that almost every one of the supporters is wearing a hat. Operating in the Birmingham League during this season, the club had a successful campaign, finishing as runners-up to Aston Villa. Their full record was: played 34, won 24, drawn 4, lost 6 (52 points); goals for 79, against 42.

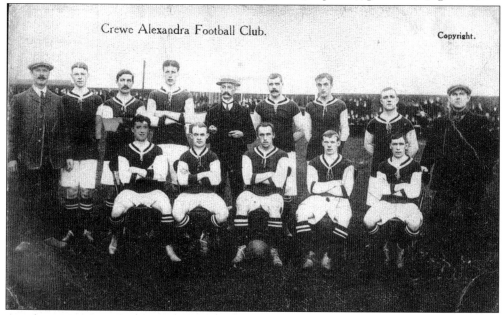

Another group from the 1908/09 season, taken at the railway end of the ground. The fencing was the familiar one of railway sleepers, which lasted many years. In the centre of the back row is the club's chairman, Mr George Hughes.

Above left: Herbert Birchenough. An excellent goalkeeper born in Haslington who, after playing for his local side, joined the famous Alex Hornets. He went on to have League experience with Port Vale, Glossop (then in Division One) and Newton Heath (later Manchester United). He returned to Crewe Alexandra in 1902 and served the club with distinction for many years. *Above right:* Bill Coventry was a keen rival to Birchenough for the 'keeper's jersey. Born in Chester, he left Crewe to join Chester but later came back to turn in many excellent performances.

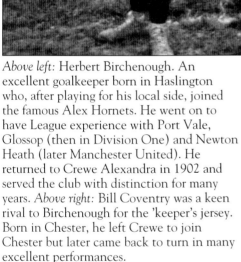

Sam Timmis was born in Audley and came to Crewe as a player from Lincoln City. He later became the trainer and served the club in that capacity for many seasons. He was also a capable cricketer.

The Crewe line-up for the 1911/12 season. From left to right, back row: W. Cunningham (Director), J. Mason, J.W. Whitehead (Referee), E. Fletcher, S. Peters, J. Barratt (Director), W. Coventry, T. Haywood, F. Stanley, S. Timmis (Trainer). Front row: A. Davis, H.E. King, W. Spittle (Captain), F.J. Chapple, H. Walley. By this time the club had moved from the Birmingham League to the Central League. Their division was headed by Lincoln City, with Port Vale in second place and the Alex in third. Below them were Everton in fourth and Liverpool in fifth position.

Football Association Cup.
Played at Bristol, Jan. 14th, 1911.
Crewe Alexandra 3.   Bristol City 0.

Saturday 14 January 1911 and a remarkable FA Cup result was achieved by the club when they defeated Bristol City 3-0; City were a Division One side at the time. The Crewe heroes who scored were Haywood, King and Chapple. The origin of the drawing is unknown.

Left: Philip Smith was a formidable centre forward and consistent marksman in his time. On one occasion he scored two hat-tricks on the same day (Christmas 1909) – one for the reserves and one for the first team. *Right:* Ernest Stansworth was a wing half who came to Crewe from Brierley Hill after previous service with West Bromwich Albion. He played most of his games at Crewe in the reserve side.

The 1910/11 season proved to be a very successful one. Crewe won the Keys Cup, Combination Championship and Cheshire Senior Cup.

It must be summer judging by the headgear worn by the ladies and gentlemen in the 'grandstand' at Gresty Road.

Action from a Birmingham League game at Gresty Road. The club flagpole is clearly visible on the Popular Side. At this time players had to come through the crowd alongside the covered part of that side of the ground to reach the pitch.

Two

Back into the League Fold
1920-1938

The reserve side operated in the Cheshire County League in 1920/21. They are pictured here in front of the covered accommodation on the Popular Side of the ground.

This page features three examples of the 'Pinnace' series of cards. These were very popular in the 1920s. Although the series comprised over 1,000 cards, only 12 featured Crewe players. To obtain bigger photographs, collectors exchanged 25 or 100 of the smaller size to obtain one of the large ones. The players shown here are W. Caulfield (top left), T. Kellett (top right) and E. Turner (left).

PROFIT AND LOSS ACCOUNT,

Season 1921—1922.

	£	s.	d.		£	s.	d.	£	s.	d.
To Players', Trainers', and Groundsmen's Wages, Expenses, &c.	5074	2	2	By Gate Money taken at Crewe	9894	13	1			
" Travelling Expenses	697	8	11	" Less Shares paid to other Clubs	1238	17	9			
" Hotel Expenses	596	9	0					8655	15	4
" Checkers, Referees, Linesmen & Police	441	13	3	" Season Ticket Money				451	10	0
" Printing, Posting and Advertising ...	146	18	9	" Subscriptions, Donations, &c.				71	16	0
" Stamps, Telegrams and Petty Cash ...	56	12	3	" Shares of Gates from other Clubs ...				464	13	0
" Telephone Rent and Calls	21	19	5	" Rent of Refreshment Booths and Hire of						
" Leagues and Associations, Subs., Fees and Forms	129	13	6	Ground				17	9	8
" Salaries and Auditor's Fees ...	170	10	0	" Transfer of Players				1000	0	0
" Expenses attending Meetings, &c. ...	56	4	9	" 20% Gates from League Clubs				754	18	3
" Rents, Rates, Taxes and Insurance ...	151	11	6					11416	2	3
" Boots, Pads, Studs and Repairs ...	43	15	2	" Loss on Season				95	16	7
" Outfitting and Repairs, also Washing ...	80	10	0							
" Footballs	9	4	6							
" Repairs to Ground and Rolling ...	62	12	9							
" Stands, Buildings and Fences—Repairs	52	2	9							
" Training Expenses and Material ...	24	14	3							
" Porterage and Sundry Charges ...	2	5	1							
" Wreath	1	1	0							
" Special Medical Fees and Expenses ...	25	15	0							
" Transfer of Players	3	0	0							
" National Insurance	18	2	2							
" Coal, Gas and Water	20	19	7							
" W.C.A. Premiums	39	1	7							
" Bank Charges	32	12	3							
" Entertainment Tax	2429	9	7							
" 20% Gates to League Clubs	750	16	3							
" Expenses re Formation of League—Div. 3	15	0	0							
" Gates—Practice Matches—										
Crewe Cottage Hospital	52	15	7							
Railway Convalescent Homes ...	46	13	2							
Ex-Servicemen's Benevolent &c. Funds	40	0	0							
Cheshire F.A. Benevolent Fund ...	20	0	0							
	11313	14	2							
" Depreciation	198	4	8							
	£11511	18	10					£11511	18	10

Auditor's Report to the Shareholders.

I have audited the Accounts of the Crewe Alexandra Football Club Company, Limited, to the 15th May, 1922, and I report that I have obtained all the information and explanations I have required, and in my opinion the above Balance Sheet of the 15th May, 1922, is properly drawn up so as to exhibit a true and correct view of the state of the Company's affairs according to the best of my information and the explanations given to me and as shewn by the Books of the Company.

HARRY H. HUGHES, Auditor.

July 10th, 1922.

The profit and loss account from the club's balance sheet that was presented to the AGM of shareholders on the 15 May 1922 following the first season in Division Three (North). Crewe were one of the founder members of this division of the Football League – the inaugural season of which ended with Stockport County as champions and the Alex in sixth place. Billy Caulfield had the honour of scoring the club's first goal in the new league on the opening day game against Tranmere.

25

Reserve team line-up for the 1922/23 season. From left to right, back row: Walker, Williamson, Allman, Cope, Wootton, Wright, Lowe (Trainer). Front row: Hassall, Purcell, Winterburn, Davies, Wagstaffe.

Members of Crewe Alexandra (left to right): Scott, Charlton, Albinson, Harrington, Birtles, Smith, Goodwin, Perry, Turner, Hassall, Hodges.

This particular Crewe Alexandra line-up appeared in the *All Sports Topical Illustrated Weekly* on 24 November 1923.

Left: Bob Dunn played five times in the 1921/22 season at centre half. His debut was on the 15 October 1921 at home to Chesterfield, a game that Crewe lost 2-1. He was born in Birmingham. *Right:* Charlie Chorlton had three League seasons with Crewe – 1921/22, 1922/23 and 1923/24. He played 65 games in the left-back position. His debut was on the 3 September 1921, at home to Tranmere Rovers.

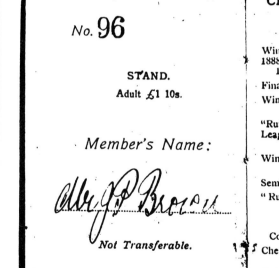

Season ticket for the 1925/26 season, issued to J.P. Brown [the author's uncle, who introduced him to Crewe Alexandra]. The price of £1 10s entitled the holder to all Division Three (North) and Cheshire League fixtures.

DEATH OF OUR SECRETARY.

It is with profound regret we have to write of the death of our Club Secretary, which occurred last Sunday, after a protracted illness, at the age of 55. Mr. J. B. Blomerley was born at Leeds, being the son of a railway guard, who served for many years on the Lancashire and Yorkshire Railway. At the age of thirteen, our secretary commenced his working career at the Goods Department, Leeds, L. and N. W. He was transferred to the Permanent Way Department, Crewe, in the year 1886, on the staff of the late Mr. Buck. On settling down in Crewe he became a member of our Football Club and was destined to play a very prominent part in its organization. It was in 1896 that Mr. Blomerley took over the Secretaryship at the request of a good number of his friends, as the club was then in financial difficulty and the ground was altogether unsuitable. Mr. Blomerley at once saw what was required and with courage and determination has brought much better football into Crewe than that of the club's early days. At the time he took up the position of secretary, Crewe Alexandra, were in the Old Combination and during his period of office he has seen the Club rise first to the Old Lancashire League, and after an experience of over three seasons to the Birmingham League. After thirteen years in this league the club transferred in 1911, to the newly-formed Central League, entering the present league, Third Division (Northern Section), in 1921. As an organiser, Mr. Blomerley, excelled, and has undoubtedly made many sacrifices for our club. During the War period he declined to accept any payment for his services, owing to the club's circumstances being somewhat straightened. Mr. George Hughes, who has been intimately acquainted with Mr. Blomerley over 23 years and was Chairman of the Alexandra in 1897 says, "His grit and determination were indomitable." In all his dealings he was the acme of fairness, his temper always of the best, and his buoyant character the finest asset the club possessed. Mr. Blomerley was respected, yes, and loved by all those whose pleasure it was to come beneath his influence, and his loss will be felt far beyond our town of Crewe. He was a member of the Cheshire County Football Association for 25 years and at one time was their Chairman, and his absolute integrity and impartiality endeared him to them all. Mr. Blomerley possessed sterling and business-like qualities as a Secretary and a leader. He was a marvel at tactfulness, a trustworthy friend, and a sportsman every inch—"God rest his soul."

Crewe Alexandra F.C.—1922-23.

ASTON VILLA v. CREWE ALEXANDRA.

SOUVENIR OF BENEFIT MATCH
—FOR—

J. B. BLOMERLEY,
SECRETARY,
after 26 years' service.
September 18th, 1922.

Above left: J.B. Blomerley died on Sunday 7 September 1924, and this obituary notice appeared in the club programme on 13 September 1924. *Right:* J.B. Blomerley, the secretary of the club, had been granted a benefit game on the 18 September 1922 at Gresty Road.

Tom Bailey succeeded to the position of secretary in 1924, having filled the position of assistant secretary for a number of years. A very capable administrator, he was well known for sporting a hat, fob watch and pipe.

A fixture card for the 1925/26 season, issued 'With the compliments of Sugden Bros' of Mill Street – this would have been an excellent advertisement for their wares.

A team group from around 1926. The players are sporting an all-white strip and are, from left to right, back row: Allman, Scott, Goodwin. Middle row: Kellett, Caulfield, Prince, Bricker, Mackey, Perry. Front row: Moss, Turner.

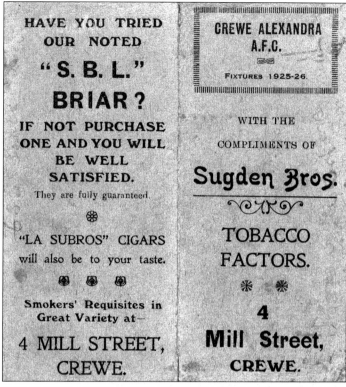

Amateur versus Professional for "The Cup." By Charles Shaw Baker.

Crewe were drawn away to London Caledonians in the FA Cup third round. The amateur side agreed to play the tie at Stamford Bridge instead of their home ground at Tufnell Park. Crewe eventually won the game 3-2. Certain details from the *Chelsea FC Chronicle* are reproduced here.

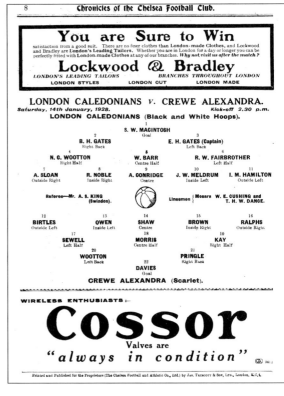

During the 1929/30 season a football legend visited Gresty Road. This picture shows Jimmy Dyer snr and Bob Roberts, a director of Manchester United, together with Billy Meredith.

Crewe Alexandra visited Villa Park to take on Aston Villa in the FA Cup on 28 January 1928. The Crewe players shown here are, from left to right, standing: Harold Kay, Harry Morris, Ben Davies, Bob Pringle, Harry Wootton. Seated: Bert Ralphs, James Brown, Vic Shaw, Jimmy Owen, Andy Blake and Freddie Birtles.

The game at Villa Park according to Norman Edwards, a cartoonist of the time. The attendance was 41,000, with 3,504 making the journey from Crewe – 1,266 paying the special fare of 4s and 2,238 taking advantage of the quarter-fare rate. At half-time Villa had only established a single goal lead, but by full-time it had become 3-0, all of the goals being netted by Cook. Consolation for the Alex came from a share of the £2,850 gate receipts.

A group of former Alex players took part in a veterans match at Gresty Road in 1931. From left to right, standing: Ike Baker (Referee), Powell (Trainer), Tommy Lowe, Was Davies, Bob Scorer, J.R. Jones, Bill Coventry, Lol Lunn, Tim Gateley, Jock Cameron, Targ Jones, Oswald Purcell, Nobby Clarke, L. Jones, Harry Hassall. Seated: Arthur Moss, Jim Hawkins, Harry Eden, J. Jones, Harry Dudley, Eli Turner, Charlie Chorlton, Wally Davies, Jack Ralphs, Tom Kellett.

Fred Keenor spent three seasons at Gresty Road, making 116 League and 5 FA Cup appearances. A former captain of Cardiff City, he had skippered their side to an FA Cup final triumph. In 1933, while at Crewe, he won his last international cap for Wales, against Scotland.

Team photograph for the 1931/32 season. From left to right, back row: Ward, Mr E. Sims Hilditch, Pringle, Dyer, Brown, Ratcliff, Maddock, Mr Wooldridge, Duthie. Front row: Murray, Deacon, Keenor, Williams, Sweeney, Weale. This season brought a reasonable sixth place final position in the division, but it had been a good year for goalscoring – the more prolific hitmen including Deacon (23), Swindells (21), Williams (17) and Sweeney (14).

A meeting with Southport at Gresty Road on the 18 November 1933 gave Bert Wright the opportunity to produce this cartoon.

Crewe v. Walsall.

Saturday, November 5th, 1932. Kick-off 2-45 p.m.

NOTE--Any alteration in either team will be notified on the Board.

CREWE

Right					Left
		Foster			
		1			
	Maddocks		Dawson		
	2		3		
	Ward	Keenor	Turner		
	4	5	6		
Murray	Deacon	Swindells	McConnell	Weale	
7	8	9	10	11	

O

Lee	Turner	Alsop	Ball	Coward
12	13	14	15	16
	Bennett	Leslie	Reed	
	17	18	19	
	Bird	Langford		
	20	21		
	Cunningham			
	22			

Left				Right

WALSALL

Referee H. N. Mee, Mansfield.

Linesmen A. E. Smith and G. Cahill

Left: On Saturday 5 November 1932, Sir Francis Joseph officially opened the new stand at Gresty Road. A souvenir programme was produced to mark the occasion. The previous stand had been destroyed by fire earlier in the year. *Right:* The team line-ups for the game against Walsall which gave Crewe a 2-1 victory, with goals from Maddock and Weale. Centre forward Alsop, whose goal knocked out Arsenal in the FA Cup, was in this Walsall side.

Players and the board of directors out on the bowling green.

Armstrong and Jackie Waring out of football kit for a change. Winger Waring is sporting his 'plus fours'.

The winners of the Welsh Cup in the 1935/36 season line up in front of the Gresty Road End goal. From left to right, back row: G. Lilleycrop (Trainer), W. Brown (Director), G. Blake, S. Burkhill (Director), J. Wilson, C. Welch (Chairman), A. Swift, G. Wooldridge (Director), C. Kneale, H. Morris (Assistant Secretary), G. Gilchrist, T. Bailey (Secretary), C. Cope (Director). Front row: J. Waring, T. Armstrong, H. Swindells, J. Scott (Captain), A. Wood, A. Rigby.

The *News Chronicle* produced the above team group for the 1936/37 season. From left to right, back row: Rigby, Waring, Wilson, Kneale, Swift, Turnbull, Scott, Reid, Wright, G. Lilleycrop (Trainer/manager). Front row: Nicol, Armstrong, Swindells, Dyer, Baldwin. It was only goal difference that saved Crewe from bottom place in the table at the end of this season. However, in the FA Cup they battled through to the third round, finally going down 0-2 at home to Plymouth Argyle in front of 11,452 fans.

Stockport-born Herbert Swindells is still the only player to have passed the 100 goal mark for Crewe. In his ten seasons with the club, he made 257 League and 14 FA Cup appearances, scoring 126 League and 6 cup goals. He made his debut in 1927/28 and stayed with the club until the 1936/37 season.

A penny was sufficient to buy a programme in 1938/39. Rochdale visited Gresty Road on Good
Friday and were beaten 4-1. The eight-page programme included many interesting
advertisements – including seats at the Kino picture house at 4d, 6d, 9d or 1s 3d.

38

Three

The War Years
and into the Sixties
1939-1961

The 1939/40 season was only two games old when war was declared on 3 September 1939. Crewe's only home fixture had been on Saturday 2 September against Hartlepool. The centre pages from the programme (shown above) were contained in a special booklet issued by the Football League, priced at 3d.

In the 1941/42 season, Crewe Alexandra were switched from the Northern to the Southern section of the League, with Stoke City moving in the opposite direction. As Crewe were unable to undertake the travelling, they withdrew and joined the North Staffs League. The team group shown here comprises, from left to right, back row: Jack Williams (Director), Wheatley, Stan Parker, Dennis Thornhill, Jack Bourne, Harry Egerton, Charlie Turnock, Harry Jones (Trainer). Front row: Eric Aldersea, Hollinshead, Coonihan, Jack Le Clere, Bob Harding.

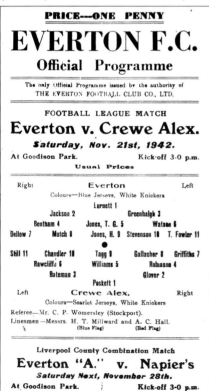

Wartime football gave the club the opportunity to play teams they would not normally meet. This example shows Crewe in opposition to Everton. The Alex lost this encounter 4-0.

Liverpool : 1

Right		Hobson		Left
	Bush 2		Gulliver 3	
	Kaye 4	Hughes 5	Pilling 6	
Shepherd 7	Dix 8	Welsh 9	Taylor 10	Campbell 11

Linesman—
E. Bailey, Hanley.

Referee—C. HALL,
Chester.

Linesman—
B. Thirlwall, Hanley.

Basnett 11	Chandler 10	Boothway 9	Robinson 8	McCormick 7
	Still 6	Hughes 5	Hill 4	
	Shaw 3		Tagg 2	
Left		Graham 1		Right

Crewe 4

see over)   Any teration in teams will be announced on board

Liverpool visited Gresty Road on Saturday 23 September 1944. An attendance of 4,440 saw the home side win 4-1.

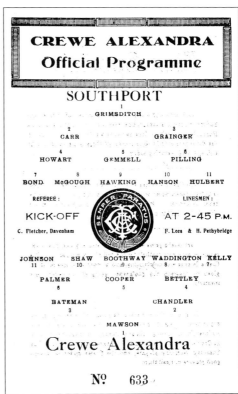

CREWE ALEXANDRA
Official Programme

SOUTHPORT

GRIMSDITCH 1

CARR 2		GRAINGER 3
HOWART 4	GEMMELL 5	PILLING 6
BOND 7	McGOUGH 8	HAWKING 9	HANSON 10	HULBERT 11

REFEREE :
KICK-OFF   AT 2-45 P.M.
C. Fletcher, Davenham

LINESMEN :
F. Lees & H. Pethybridge

JOHNSON 11	SHAW 10	BOOTHWAY 9	WADDINGTON 8	KELLY 7
PALMER 6		COOPER 5		BETTLEY 4
BATEMAN 3				CHANDLER 2

MAWSON 1

Crewe Alexandra

Nº 633

The last of the wartime seasons was 1945/46. On 22 January 1946, Southport were the visitors to Gresty Road. The gate for the game was 3,195 and the match ended all square at 1-1. A note on the reverse side reads 'The Chairman and Manager were up North last Saturday watching players and the Crewe policy is to sign good players not sell them'.

41

A team line-up from the 1947/48 season. From left to right, back row: Dowey, Micklewright, Evans, Lindsay, Barlow, Bossons. Front row: Byrne, Morris, Basford, Fletcher, Jones, Jimmy Dyer.

Sheffield United came to Gresty Road for an FA Cup third round tie on 10 January 1948. Bob Finan (2) and Eric Jones gave Crewe a 3-1 win. Louis Ollier produced this caricature of the team, which was used in the match programme.

Toughening up training prior to the 1948/49 season. From left to right: Jack Basford carrying Jack Meaney, Frank Mitcheson with Roy Phillips, Bob Young with Ken Linstrem, Fred Inskip with Tony Waddington, Peter Ellson with Albert Parker and Tommy Briggs with Danny Smith.

A confident looking squad pose for the photographer prior to the 1949/50 season. From left to right, back row: Archie Capper (Trainer), Albert Parker, Tony Waddington, Peter Ellson, Roy Hodgson, Bob Young, Jack Meaney, Arthur Turner (Manager). Front row: David Campbell, Albert Mullard, Roy Phillips, Frank Mitcheson, Danny Smith.

The Permanent Way ground was the venue for this group of players, many of whom played in the Cheshire League side. From left to right, back row: J. Dyer, A. Turner (Manager), C. Hardstaff, Clews, R. Walton, G. Roberts, H. Taylor, A. Waddington. Middle row: H. Maden, G. Cooke, N. Wakefield, C. Maddox, J. Sinclair, C. Fox, G. Price. Front row: L. Mills, B. Hough, E. Morris, S. Morris, B. Hassall.

The Crewe Alexandra reserve side photographed at Hyde United on Saturday 24 December 1949. From left to right, standing: W. Banks (Director), Eric Hornby, Don Footitt, Gordon Cooke, Jack Basford, Jack Rothwell, J. Dyer (Trainer), Tom Doig (Assistant Secretary). Seated: David Mountford, Alec Hamilton, Les Micklewright, Cecil Hardstaff, Harold Barlow, Johnnie King.

The first team squad still has a familiar look in the 1950/51 season. This group was taken at Rochdale and the players are, from left to right, back row: Albert Parker, Peter Ellson, Bob Young, Tony Waddington, Jack Meaney. Front row: Roy Phillips, Frank Mitcheson, Tommy Briggs, Jack Basford, Danny Smith, Jimmy McGuigan.

The old baths in the home dressing room in 1951/52. Posing for the cameraman on this occasion are, from left to right: Albert Parker, Jack Basford, Peter Ellson, Jack Meaney, Bob Young, Peter Cook, Danny Smith and Jimmy McGuigan.

Led by Jimmy McGuigan, Jack Meaney and Reg Chapman, the players go on a training run, despite the conditions, in the 1951/52 season. Keeping a watchful eye on them are manager Arthur Turner and trainer Archie Capper.

Archie Capper watches Arthur Turner giving instructions. Jimmy McGuigan, Peter Cook, Don Travis, Jack Basford and Danny Smith are listening intently.

46

Still in the 1951/52 season, the snow-covered ground is being fully utilised by the thirteen players and their trainer, Archie Capper.

Left: Always referred to as the 'Railway Policeman' (his former profession), Peter Ellson was a fearless 'keeper for the Alex. He played in goal in 219 League games for the club. *Right:* Frank Blunstone originally joined the club on the ground staff. His talent was soon spotted by Chelsea, who secured his signature in 1953. During his time at Chelsea he was capped by England.

Tom Doig bids farewell to Frank Blunstone in October 1953. The latter was en route to sign for Chelsea for a record fee of £8,000. Frank scored on his Chelsea debut in a 3-2 win at Tottenham.

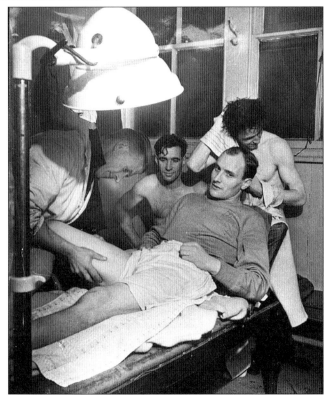

Receiving treatment under trainer Archie Capper is Jack Meaney, watched by Peter Cook while Jimmy McGuigan dries his hair.

Now under new management, the 1953/54 squad enjoy a brief respite from training. From left to right, back row: Jimmy McGuigan, Billy Mould, Jack Basford, R. Delucchi (Director), Eddie Lyons, David Boyle, Frank Mitcheson. Middle row: Alf Lees, Ralph Ward (Manager), Frank Cottrell (Chairman), Danny Murphy (Captain). Front row: Eric Betts, Jack Meaney, Johnny King.

Jack Such is the trainer getting the attention of this group of players in 1954. Alongside Such is Bill Caton, while the trio in the centre is made up of Alf Lees, Peter Ellson and Angus McLean.

On 30 November 1953, Jack Meaney had to attend an FA hearing. This was because of an incident in the game against Southport on 3 October 1953, when Meaney struck Billingham. Although Jack received a suspension, they both shook hands after the hearing.

Willie Cook, formerly of Everton, took over the managerial reins from Maurice Lindley on 23 December 1956. Despite his efforts the club were unable to get out of the re-election zone and he left Crewe in the summer of 1957.

Johnny Kelly joined the club from
Third Lanark during the 1959/60
season. He is pictured here signing
on, watched by manager Harry Ware
and secretary Peter Robinson.

Eric and Beryl Barnes are pictured at
home, discussing the possibility of a
move to Leeds United. The move
never took place and he went in to
claim the Crewe centre half spot for
many seasons.

September 1959 and Geoff Morgans 'signs on the dotted line' for the Alex, watched by his father and secretary Peter Robinson.

Chris Riley finds his way through the Spurs defence to score the equalizing goal at Gresty Road. The 2-2 final score gave the Alex a replay at White Hart Lane.

Following the 2-2 draw at home to Spurs on Saturday 30 January 1960, demand for replay tickets was keen. As can be seen in this picture, the fans queued in orderly fashion. Expectations for the game were high, but a 10-1 scoreline at half-time finally finished 13-2 in Spurs' favour. The attendance of 64,365 for the game, played on 3 February 1960, is still the largest crowd the Alex have ever played in front of.

Just one of the many FA Cup replay tickets that were eagerly snapped up by the Crewe supporters. Several special trains were laid on to take fans to White Hart Lane.

53

Left: Billy Stark was a member of the Crewe side which won at Chelsea on the 6 February 1961 and the scorer of one of the goals on that never-to-be-forgotten day. *Right:* Alan Foster was also a member of the Alex side at Stamford Bridge. Although he did not score on that occasion, he contributed some useful goals during his time at Gresty Road.

Billy Stark's header gives Crewe the lead in the cup tie against Chelsea at Stamford Bridge in front of a crowd of 32,574.

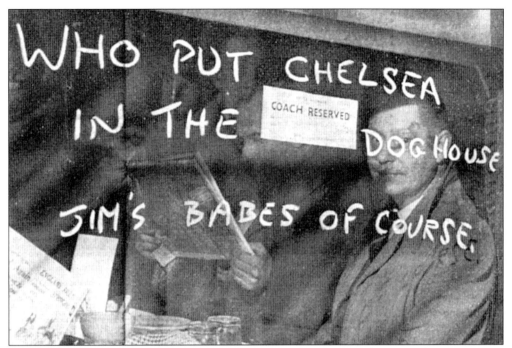

A poignant message on the window of a compartment of the train bringing the Crewe team back from London after beating Chelsea. This was published in the *Sunday Dispatch* of 6 February 1961.

Fate paired Crewe yet again with Spurs in the FA Cup in 1961. This brilliant Waite cartoon needs little explanation. The second meeting with Spurs in the FA Cup saw Crewe go down 5-1. Terry Tighe scored the Crewe goal – thus winning a bet with his former schoolfriend, Dave Mackay, who was in the Spurs line-up.

The Crewe squad ready to take on the mighty Spurs. From left to right, back row: Stan Keery, Brian Williamson, Eric Barnes, Jimmy Shepherd, Alan Foster, Jimmy McGill. Front row: Billy Stark, Terry Tighe, Don Campbell, Barrie Wheatley, Merfyn Jones.

Don Campbell, followed by 'keeper Brian Williamson, leads the Crewe side out at White Hart Lane. Although defeated 5-1 they made many friends in the capital and the heroics performed by Billy Williamson in the Crewe goal are well remembered by the Crewe fans.

Four

Promotion Twice but also Relegation
1962-1982

Relaxing with some golfing practice at the Crewe Golf Club are Dusty Miller, Brian Williamson, Jimmy Shepherd, Billy Haydock, Frank Lord and the club professional.

Do you remember the old entrance to the Gresty Road ground? Dennis McGarrigle signs an autograph for a young fan and, on the right, what in 1961 served as the secretary's office.

The 1962/63 first team squad were a fine body of men. From left to right, back row: Stan Keery, Peter Leigh, Geoff Hickson, Dave Ewing, Les Riggs, Frank Lord. Front row: Billy Haydock, Barrie Wheatley, Dave Whelan, Johnny King, Ron Smith.

The Alex in action at Stockport on 1 September 1962. This goalbound effort was not from Johnny King, who is pictured, but Billy Haydock (out of camera shot).

Non-League opposition, in the form of Scarborough, came to Gresty Road on 3 November 1962 and gained a 1-1 draw. Scarborough 'keeper Quairney claims the ball close to the line.

Ronnie Smith scores the Crewe goal in a 1-1 draw at Belle Vue, home of Doncaster Rovers, on 18 May 1963.

Frank Lord causing problems in the Oldham defence in the League fixture which ended Crewe 2 Oldham Athletic 3.

Brian Hassall (still clutching his rattle) dashes onto the Gresty Road pitch after Frank Lord had scored the winner against Exeter City on 22 May 1963 – the Alex had won promotion at last! Ronnie Smith, Les Riggs and Barrie Wheatley are also pictured.

Hundreds of happy faces as the Crewe fans invade Gresty Road following that 1-0 win over Exeter City. A few of the fans can be spotted with old-fashioned rattles.

Bath time celebrations after the Exeter game: Barrie Wheatley, Dave Whelan, Stan Keery, Peter Leigh, Frank Lord, Les Riggs, Jimmy Shepherd and Johnny King are enjoying a good soak.

The final team group of the promotion-winning 1962/63 season side. From left to right, back row: Stan Keery, Ronnie Smith. Middle row: Peter Leigh, Jimmy Shepherd, Geoff Hickson, Dave Ewing, Les Riggs. Front row: Billy Haydock, Barrie Wheatley, Dave Whelan, Frank Lord, Johnny King.

Division Three action with Wrexham visiting Gresty Road on 21 March 1964. The Wrexham 'keeper Fleet is just managing to palm clear a shot from Peter Gowans.

The old stand at Valley Parade, Bradford, provides the backdrop for this photograph. Mick Gannon and Ralph Marshall can only watch as the ball enters the net in a 5-2 defeat.

The 1965/66 squad line up in front of the main stand. From left to right, back row: Tecwyn Jones, Ralph Marshall, Eric Barnes, Willie Mailey, Peter Leigh, Norman Bodell, Dave Whelan. Front row: Peter Gowans, Peter Kane, Johnny King, Alan Bradshaw, Barrie Wheatley, David Finch (mascot).

Left: Geoff Hickson pictured in mid-air action during training at the Railway End. Geoff made a total of 106 League appearances for the Alex. *Right:* Johnny King started and finished his career at Crewe Alexandra. He also had several seasons with Stoke City and a short spell with Cardiff City. Johnny played a total of 227 League games for the Alex.

When Ernie Tagg took over as manager for the first time he gave up his milk round. This cartoon illustrates how the news was interpreted by Roy Ullyett.

Trevor Porteous and Ernie Tagg flank a poster advertising the FA Cup fourth round tie between Crewe Alexandra and Coventry City at Gresty Road to be played on Saturday 12 February 1966. Crewe almost produced a shock result in this cup match as they led 1-0 until Rees scored an injury time Coventry equaliser. Coventry ran out comfortable 4-1 winners in the replay at Highfield Road.

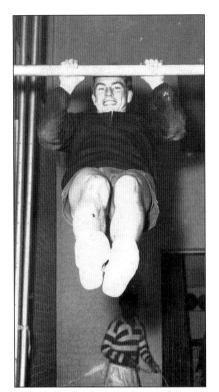 

Left: John Mahoney thoroughly enjoying his exercises on the bar in the gymnasium. *Right:* Ralph Marshall, on the ground, views John Mahoney from a different perspective.

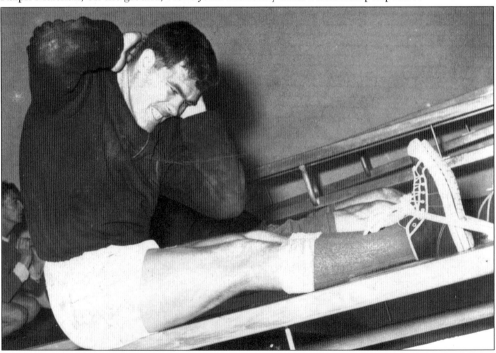

Alex 'keeper Willie Mailey makes full use of the bench for some stretching exercises.

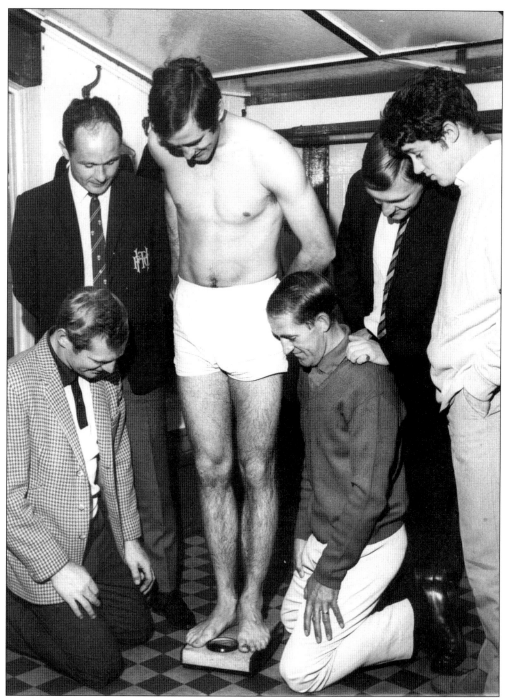

It's weigh-in time with John Regan on the scales, watched intently by Peter Leigh, Kevin McHale (still sporting his Huddersfield blazer), Gordon Wallace, Alan Tarbuck and Don Ratcliffe.

The Crewe Alexandra squad are all ready for the 1969/70 season. From left to right, back row: John Inglis, Roy Gater, Willie Mailey, Ernie Adams, Tommy Lowry, Steve Arnold. Middle row: Alan A'Court (Assistant Manager/Coach), Mick Gill (Physiotherapist), Albert Harley, Neil Turner, Eric Barnes, Ivan Hollett, Keith Stott, David Miller, Peter Higgins, Joe Maloney (Trainer). Front row: Stephen Wilkinson, Gordon Wallace, Mick Gannon, John McHugh (Chairman), Ernie Tagg (Manager), Kevin McHale, Pat Morrissey, Peter Leigh, Alan Tarbuck.

Saturday 13 February 1971 and Lincoln City visit Gresty Road only to return home pointless, after losing 3-1. Stan Bowles is pictured here heading one of the Crewe goals.

Welcoming the new boy – Peter Higgins is on the left with manager Ernie Tagg, Peter Leigh, chairman Norman Rowlinson and Neil Turner.

Crewe-born Ernie Tagg joined the club in October 1937. An inside forward, he was transferred to Wolves in May 1938, later moving to Bournemouth and finally to Carlisle. Ernie was trainer at the club during the time that Ralph Ward was manager. He became manager himself in 1964 and came back again in that capacity on two more occasions, also serving as a member of the board of directors. Now in his eighties, Ernie still watches games at Gresty Road, where he is an honorary life vice-president.

Another team group, this time from the 1970/71 season. From left to right, back row: Glyn Osborne, Tommy Lowry, Steve Arnold, Ernie Adams, Ivan Hollett, Alan Bradshaw, Les Wain. Front row: Paul Hince, Kevin McHale, Peter Leigh, Roy Gater, Pat Morrissey. It was seventeenth place for the Alex at the end of this campaign, with 'keeper Ernie Adams and wing half Roy Gater making maximum appearances. Pat Morrisey topped the scorers for the club in the League with 20, followed by Stan Bowles with 13 and Alan Bradshaw with 10.

Crewe's only game in the Watney Cup was against Carlisle United on Saturday 31 July 1971. Crewe lost the game 3-1: the scorer for the Alex was Tommy Lowry (hidden from view). That strike was one of only three goals scored in all his years at Crewe.

Aerial action in the Peterborough goalmouth at Gresty Road on 19 February 1972. Michael Drewery, the visitors' 'keeper, clears despite the attention of Hughen Riley and Keith East.

The team pose for a group photograph at Elm Park (Reading) on the opening day of the 1972/73 season. From left to right, back row: John Manning, Roy Gater, Geoff Crudgington, Alan Gillett, Tommy Lowry, Alan Kelley. Front row: Terry Nicholl, Hughen Riley, Alan Bradshaw, Arthur Peat, Gerry Humphreys, Les Wain.

A star visitor in the dressing room at Luton on 13 January 1973 for the FA Cup third round tie. Pictured, from left to right, are: Tommy Lowry, Jimmy Melia (Manager), Terry Nicholl, Eric Morecambe, Phil Nicholls, Alan Tewley, Dave Gillett and Hughen Riley.

Lincoln City 'keeper Peter Grotier faces his own goal with a look of despair as Dennis Nelson slots in an injury-time winner on 24 August 1974.

Hughen Riley celebrates his goal against Doncaster Rovers with some young fans at the Gresty Road end of the ground on 21 September 1974. Crewe won the game 2-1.

Secretary Chris Jones with the Crewe players prior to a meeting with the FA regarding contracts in 1975 at the Royal Hotel. The players are: Hughie Reed, Dennis Nelson, Bernard Purdie, Michael Evans, Paul Bevan, Dai Davies, Phil Nicholls, Tommy Lowry, Paul Bowles, Tommy Maguire, Paul Antrobus, Alan Kelley and Hughie Cheetham.

The first ever Manager of the Month accolade awarded to a Crewe manager. Jimmy Melia celebrates the award before the League Cup second round game against Birmingham City on 11 September 1974.

Liverpool-born record breaker Tommy Lowry joined the Alex staff in the summer of 1966. He first appeared in the Alex colours on 19 October 1966, for the home game against Lincoln City. The match only lasted 27 minutes, as a floodlight failure caused the game to be abandoned with Crewe losing 1-0. His official debut was against Southend United on the 22 October 1966 and his final game for Crewe was at Scunthorpe on 23 August 1977. In all he played in 481 first team games for Crewe – 453 League, 24 League Cup, 21 FA Cup and 1 Watney Cup. This is a record that may well stand the test of time.

A vital goal for Crewe as Gerry Humphreys slots home the winning goal from the penalty spot against Steve Sherwood of Chelsea in 1975. The game was a League Cup second round tie which Crewe won 1-0. Crewe had earned their place in this round after defeating Tranmere Rovers 2-1 in extra-time in a three-match tie. Following the triumph over Chelsea, the Alex were to play Tottenham Hotspur at Gresty Road. Unfortunately, the game finished as a 2-0 away win for the Londoners.

A completely relaxed Dai Davies, Paul Bowles, Tommy Lowry, and Gerry Humphreys chat to new signing Wyn Davies at the start of the 1976/77 season.

Geoff Crudgington at full stretch in a training session. Signed from Aston Villa, firstly on loan, then on a permanent basis, he made 137 consecutive appearances in the Crewe goal between 17 August 1974 and 19 February 1977.

A successful penalty conversion – Ray Lugg's shot beats the outstretched fingertips of Terry Gennoe of Halifax on 16 October 1976.

Wyn Davies in action against Scunthorpe United on 12 October 1977.

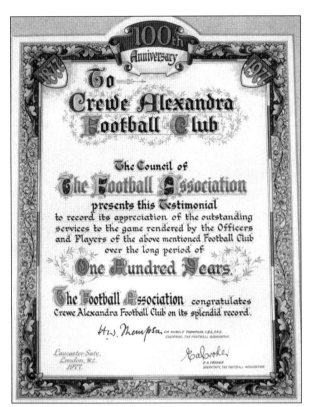

The club celebrated its 100th anniversary in 1977 and they were presented with this illuminated scroll to mark the occasion – this now occupies a prominent place at Gresty Road.

In the 1977/78 season, the club were able to sign Peter Coyne as the result of an appeal made in the town. Chaiman Norman Rowlinson watches Harry Gregg receive a cheque from the appeal's organizer.

David Felgate, on loan to Crewe from Bolton, in the thick of the action at Somerton Park, then the home of Newport County, in a League encounter on 10 November 1979.

Portsmouth made their first-ever visit to Gresty Road on the 11 November 1978. Peter Mellor is seen collecting the ball as Ian Roberts challenges.

A windy day for the 1979/80 pre-season team photograph. From left to right, back row: Neil Wilkinson, Danny Bowers, Dai Davies, Paul Bevan, Kevin Rafferty, Paul Bowles, Bob Scott, Mike Tune, Richard Wainwright. Middle row: Kevin Lewis, Peter Coyne, Ian Ashworth, Bernard Purdie, Warwick Rimmer (Assistant Manager/Coach), Geoff Hunter, Dennis Nelson, Garry Dulson. Front row: Steve Hanlon, Carl Evans.

The weather causes problems at times and, prior to the home game against Hereford on 23 February 1980, groundsman Tony Lawrence (centre) marks the lines with Richard Wainwright (left) and Kevin Rafferty (right) clearing straw from the pitch.

Bruce Grobbelaar made his League debut in English football with Crewe Alexandra at Wigan on the 21 December 1979. He played in all the remaining games that season and, in the final game, scored a penalty in the 2-0 win over York City. This makes him the only Crewe 'keeper to have scored in a League game to date.

Following the final game of the 1979/80 season on 5 May 1980, the fans came onto the pitch, despite the fact that the team had failed to get out of the re-election zone.

Crewe Alexandra squad, 1980/81. From left to right, back row: Jimmy Dyer (Physiotherapist), John McMahon, Terry Conroy, Bob Scott, Ken Mulhearn, Colin Chesters, Mick Guy, Colin Prophett (Player/Coach). Middle row: Danny Bowers, Kevin Lewis, Neil Wilkinson, Tony Waddington (Manager), Dennis Nelson (Captain), Geoff Hunter, Dai Davies. Front row: Steve Hanlon, Carl Evans, Peter Coyne.

Left: Peter Coyne leaves the field at Gresty Road, having scored four goals against Hereford United on 7 October 1980. Peter later received a television set as a reward for his scoring feat. *Right:* Ian Callaghan, for so long a star at Anfield, ended his League career with Crewe in the 1981/82 season. He made a total of 17 League and cup appearances. He played his last League game at Halifax on 20 March 1982.

Many footballers have an ambition to play on all the 92 League grounds during their career. Most do not realise that ambition, but on Saturday 7 February 1981 Colin Prophett managed it. His final ground was Plough Lane, home of Wimbledon FC, hence the poster proclaiming his '92 not out'. Colin was born in Crewe in 1947 and had played reserve team football with the Alex before joining Sheffield Wednesday in 1968. He finished his career at Gresty Road, his full appearance record being: Sheffield Wednesday 111 (7 goals), Norwich City 34 (0), Swindon Town 158 (10), Chesterfield 35 (1), Crewe Alexandra 79 (1). The only goal Colin scored for his home town team was at home in the game against Wigan Athletic on 13 December 1980, when they lost 2-1.

Arfon Griffiths MBE took over from Tony Waddington and is shown here with his players. From left to right, back row: Sean Haslegrave, David Goodwin, Daryl Chapman, Tony Moore, Peter Craven, Owen Brown. Middle row: Danny Bowers, Bernard Purdie, Nick Longley, Bob Scott, Steve Smith, Clive Evans, Mel Sutton, Neil Salathiel. Front row: Arfon Griffiths.

Faced with a goalkeeper crisis for the away game at Darlington on the 4 April 1982 (due to Ken Mulhearn having a back injury), Colin Chesters, who was normally a centre forward, donned the green jersey. He saved a penalty but the Alex still lost 1-0.

84

Five
Into the Dario Era
1983-1993

A new manager, Dario Gradi, joined the club in the summer of 1983 and his squad pose here for the annual photocall ritual. From left to right, back row: Mark Leonard, Nigel Hart, Steve Smith, Nick Longley, Garry Blissett, Steve Davis, Jimmy Dyer (Physiotherapist). Middle row: Paul Brady, Steve Willshaw, Dave Pullar, Dario Gradi (Manager), Bob Scott, Dave Waller, Danny Bowers, Steve Edwards. Front row: Paul Spittle, Tony Cliss, Peter King, John Crabbe.

Two working and one watching in the gymnasium: Steve Davis, Dave Waller and Steve Saunders make use of the equipment.

John Pemberton in aerial action at Ninian Park Cardiff on 4 October 1986. Steve Davis, Phil Power and Garry Blissett can also be seen in the photograph.

A typical strike by centre forward Dave Waller during his time at Gresty Road.

Geoff Thomas scores with this diving header against his former club Rochdale in a 5-1 win on 31 March 1987.

When Crewe visited Molineux in January 1987, the bottom tier of the stand was not in use, hence the absence of supporters. A Peter Bodak hat-trick gave Crewe a 3-2 win.

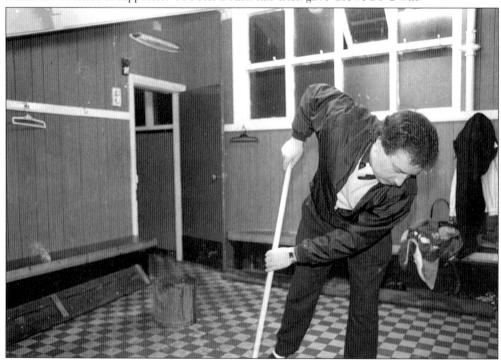

Towards the end of the 1986/87 season, the home and away dressing rooms were taken out of use and replaced. Russell Hickton is seen 'mopping up' after a game.

Saturday 9 May 1987 saw a dramatic final game at Torquay. An Alsatian dog played its part in the drama as Crewe drew 2-2. It was also a farewell appearance for Geoff Thomas, who joined Crystal Palace for £60,000 at the end of the season.

The area behind the old main stand was to be cleared to make way for an Astroturf pitch in the 1986/87 season. Assistant groundsman John Talbot receives help from the players, from left to right: Steve Davis, Terry Milligan, Tony Jarvis, Rob Powner, Peter Bodak, Brian Parkin, Geoff Thomas, John Gannon, Steve Wright, Gary Blissett.

The opening day of the 1987/88 season saw the game against Bolton Wanderers switched to Burnden Park, because of ground alterations at Gresty Road. David Platt strikes to make the Crewe supporters happy as they earn a 1-1 draw.

A snowy welcome to the North East as Crewe go to Scarborough on 5 March 1988. Crewe failed to master the conditions and they lost 2-0.

It's FA Cup time again and Crewe make the short journey to Stafford. Part of the fencing collapsed at Marston Road, but these Crewe fans remained in their places.

Action from the Stafford cup tie on 19 November; Dennis Cronin scored for Crewe but the non-League side fought back to draw 2-2.

A Saturday morning kick-off for the FA Cup second round tie at Runcorn on 10 December 1988 and a Mark Gardiner strike sees Crewe are on their way to a 3-0 victory. Crewe were the first team to know they were through to the third round.

Office staff had a busy time coping with the demand for tickets for the third round game against Aston Villa. A full house was guaranteed for 7 January 1989.

Martin Spink, the Villa 'keeper, looks on helplessly as a Mark Gardiner shot enters the net to put Crewe in the lead. Villa won a very exciting game 3-2.

Club chairman John Bowler hands England Youth caps to Rob Jones (left) and Steve Walters (right).

Paul Clayton joined Crewe for £15,000 from Darlington and is pictured here making his debut on 28 January 1989 against his old club at Feethams.

Tucking into a meal at the Alexandra club are Mark Gardiner, Ian Macowat, Aaron Callaghan and Dale Jasper. Kenny Swain is looking on.

Not just an end of season game at Tranmere as promotion depended on the result. Andy Sussex, as always, is in the thick of the action, although he did not score in this vital match.

A view from the dugout at Tranmere on 13 May 1989. Phil Blakemore and Dario Gradi look on anxiously while Dennis Cronin (head bowed) cannot bear to watch.

A delighted Paul Clayton just after scoring the equaliser at Prenton Park. This goal proved sufficient to give Crewe a point, which meant they finished third and gained promotion. This meant that they finished the season with 78 points and in the third automatic promotion place, one point ahead of Scunthorpe United. Doncaster Rovers, Rotherham United and York City were the only teams to win at Crewe that season. Ever-present Paul Fishenden ended up as leading scorer, with 17 goals.

Part of the large crowd at Tranmere. Some had hoped for a higher vantage point, but eventually they were persuaded to come down.

The 1989/90 squad ready for action in Division Two. From left to right, back row: Dale Jasper, Jason Smart, Aaron Callaghan, Paul Fishenden, Paul Edwards, Andy Sussex, Paul Dyson, Chris Cutler, Paul Clayton. Middle row: Mark Gardiner, Aidan Murphy, Kenny Swain, Paul R. Edwards, Steve Walters, Rob Jones, Graham Easter. Front row: Rob Edwards, Craig Hignett, Colin Rose.

The Kop End at St Andrews, home of Birmingham City, 19 August 1989. Crewe fans greet their team for the opening game in Division Two.

Kenny Swain, Crewe's assistant manager, in action at Birmingham. Before retiring from playing, Kenny completed at least 100 games for five different clubs and also claimed the record as Crewe's oldest player, when he appeared at 39 years, 281 days.

A late substitution brings Francis Joseph into the action against Preston North End on 24 March 1990. It pays off as he heads the winner in a 1-0 victory.

David Platt returns to Gresty Road to present Dario with an England jersey. His first international appearance was against Italy in November 1989 and he went on to win 62 caps for England.

A pre-season game with Spanish side Real Valladolid at Gresty Road: Rob Jones prepares to take on Francisco Cuaresma.

The picture tells its own story – Rob Edwards, Craig Hignett and Mark Gardiner (nos 8, 9 and 10) all score in a 3-1 win at Bury in September 1990.

April 1991 and Crewe lose 1-0 at Brentford, despite the fact that, as this photograph shows, a Crewe effort was actually over the line. Crewe's claims for a goal were turned down by the referee.

Another opening day game, and Barnet's first in the Football League, 17 August 1991. Ron Futcher celebrates his first goal for Crewe and Crewe go on to win 7-4.

Barry Fry is surrounded by the press after that 7-4 defeat by Crewe at the Underhill Stadium. The attendance of 5,090 still stands as Barnet's highest attendance for a League game.

A Rumbelows League Cup first round game at Gresty Road provides the occasion for this shot. Opponents Doncaster Rovers were caught in a traffic jam, the start was delayed and the Crewe players and Dario relaxed on the pitch before the game.

No room for traffic on Gresty Road as Crewe fans queue for FA Cup tickets for the third round tie with Liverpool. When the game was played, it was Crewe's first live appearance on television.

Former colleagues, now in opposition, Rob Edwards and Rob Jones in the televised FA Cup tie from Gresty Road on 6 January 1992.

Crewe were drawn against West Ham United in the Coca Cola Cup during the 1992/93 season. The two sides drew 0-0 at Upton Park and the tie was finely poised for the second leg back in Crewe. Two goals in the last 18 minutes of the game, from Naylor (72) and Hignett (79), gave the Alex a shock win and put them through to the third round. Unfortunately their progress was halted there, as they were beaten 1-0 by Nottingham Forest.

The moment a club record was created – Tony Naylor scores his fifth goal in a 7-1 victory over Colchester United in April 1993.

May 1993 saw Crewe win their way to a Wembley appearance against York City. The Crewe players listen intently to Dario and Kenny Swain at Bisham Abbey.

Still at Bisham Abbey, Dario watches Mark Smith going into a training routine. Other players shown are Neil Lennon, Jimmy Harvey and Ashley Ward.

Making their way to the centre at Wembley are the match officials, managers, teams and mascots prior to the final against York City on 22 May 1993. A sixth place finish in the divisional table meant that Crewe were paired with Walsall in the play-off semi-final. A 9-3 aggregate scoreline saw the Alex go into the final against York City at Wembley. The tie was still scoreless at the end of normal time and York scored first in extra-time. However, Dave McKearney scored an equaliser from the penalty spot and the game went into a shoot-out. Unfortunately, Gareth Walley had his penalty saved and York were the team to win promotion.

If only it had counted! This Tony Naylor effort found its way past Dean Kiely and into the net only to be disallowed for offside.

Six

More Promotion
Campaigns and Progress
1994-1999

The TV cameras come to Gresty Road in April 1994 as the promotion battle intensifies.
Wycombe Wanderers were the visitors and a double from Ashley Ward secured the points.

With 69 minutes of the game at the Deva Stadium gone, Ashley Ward prepares to crash home the winning goal in a 2-1 victory over Chester that secured the third promotion place.

The Crewe bench at Chester as the minutes tick away. Dario's hand signals indicate – 'just keep it calm lads' – as a youthful Seth Johnson watches anxiously.

Neil Lennon gives a post-match interview on the pitch at the Deva Stadium.

Who cares about the state of dress or undress in the dressing room at Chester following the victory on 7 May 1994.

The players and officials display their promotion medals at the start of the 1994/95 season. The players shown are, from left to right: Mark Smith, Ashley Ward, Steve Macauley, Darren Rowbotham, Shaun Smith, Steve Garvey, Gareth Whalley, Wayne Collins, Martyn Booty and Steve Walters. Secretary Gill Palin, chairman John Bowler and Dario are also wearing their medals with pride.

The first of four successive Fair Play Awards presented to the club at the start of the 1994/95 season. Dario receives the trophy from Gordon Taylor of the PFA, watched by Chris Walters, the club's community officer.

One way to celebrate a goal – Robbie Savage shows his delight after scoring the only goal of the game at Brighton on 18 February 1995.

A rare win at Bradford City: Ashley Ward scores the first in a game that finished as a 2-0 away victory.

The start of an international career: manager Dario Gradi presents Robbie Savage with his Welsh Under-21 international cap in front of the home fans at Gresty Road.

A tussle for possession between Neil Lennon and a Blackpool defender in the League encounter at Bloomfield Road in late September 1995.

The temperature at Adams Park was over 100 degrees as Wycombe and Crewe met on the opening day of the 1995/96 season. Robbie Savage is pictured attempting to force his way through.

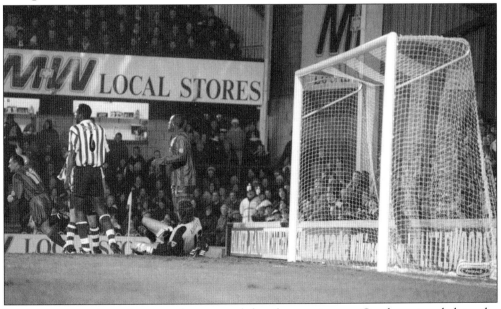

In a game staged at the second attempt (after frozen pipes at Southampton led to the postponement of the original tie), Crewe take on Southampton at the Dell. Dave Beasant is disconsolate as Rob Edwards puts Crewe into the lead.

At a prearranged signal, the Burnley fan's protest against the management begins at Turf Moor. The Alex provided the opposition for the game during which this took place, on 10 February 1996. Not all the fans turned their backs on the action.

Two Smiths in action down at the Goldstone Ground, Brighton. Peter Smith of Brighton and Shaun Smith of Crewe took part in a game that ended all square at 2-2.

Dele Adebola rises head and shoulders above the Peterborough defenders on a visit to London Road on 16 March 1996.

Due to a tremendous downpour and a thunderstorm, the team photograph for the 1996/97 season saw the players lining up under cover in the stand. From left to right, back row: Lee Ellison, Steve Pope, Lee Cox, Brian Launders, Neil Cutler, Mark Gayle, Jake Leberl, Kevin Street, James Collins, Billy Barr. Middle row: Fran Tierney, Dele Abebola, Robbie Savage, Gareth Whalley, Steve Garvey, Ashley Westwood, Shaun Smith, Lee Unsworth, Chris Lightfoot, Jamie Moralee. Front row: Steve Macauley, Danny Murphy, John Fleet (Kit Man), Steve Holland (Youth Coach), Neil Baker (Assistant Manager), Dario Gradi (Manager), Colin Little, Mark Rivers.

Gareth Whalley receives the PFA Fair Play Award from Graham Taylor at the start of the 1996/97 season.

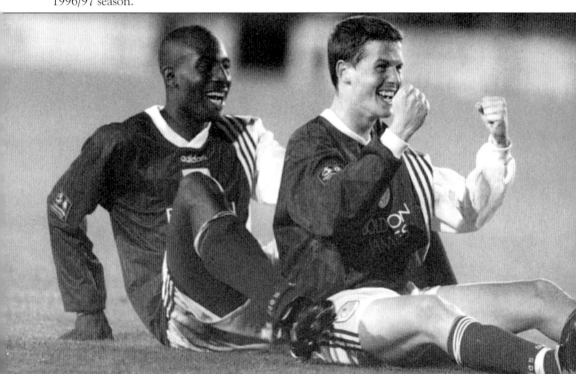

A different way to celebrate a goal: Mark Rivers is the scorer and is pictured with Dele Adebola in the home game against Blackpool on 1 October 1996.

Stretching exercises are the order of the day as Danny Murphy and Mark Rivers prepare for the game at Shrewsbury on 17 October 1996.

Difficult conditions – both to play in and photograph. The fog persisted at Hull on 7 December 1996 in this FA Cup second round, which Crewe won 5-1.

Ashley Westwood prepares to leap over the Luton 'keeper in this League encounter at Kenilworth Road in December 1996.

At the end of the 1996/97 season, John Huxley received the Division Two Groundsman of the Year Award. The Gresty Road playing surface is testimony to the care he gives it.

Shaun Smith, out of shot, brings the scores level at Kenilworth Road in the second leg of the play-off semi-final. The one goal margin from the game at Crewe proved decisive.

After the final whistle at Luton, the players and the walking wounded show their delight at winning through to another Wembley final. The players are, from left to right: Danny Murphy, Phil Charnock, Steve Garvey, Colin Little, Shaun Smith, Ashley Westwood, Chris Lightfoot, Seth Johnson, Gareth Whalley, Lee Unsworth and Steve Macauley.

May 25 1997 saw Wembley Stadium welcome Crewe Alexandra and Brentford for the Division Two play-off final.

The Crewe players and Dario wait on the pitch for the official presentation of the teams to take place prior to kick-off.

A sight to remember – the massed banners and flags of the Crewe supporters at the play-off final.

Ten minutes before half time and the lethal left foot of Shaun Smith fires in a goal for Crewe. This gave the Alex their deserved 1-0 victory over Brentford.

Mark Rivers causes problems for the Brentford defenders on a glorious afternoon at Wembley.

The substitutions have taken place and the tension mounts. Expressions on the individuals' faces tell their own stories.

Following the long climb up the steps, Gareth Whalley lifts the trophy. Alongside him are Danny Murphy, Steve Garvey, Colin Little and Ashley Westwood. Chairman John Bowler and his wife show their delight at the team's achievement.

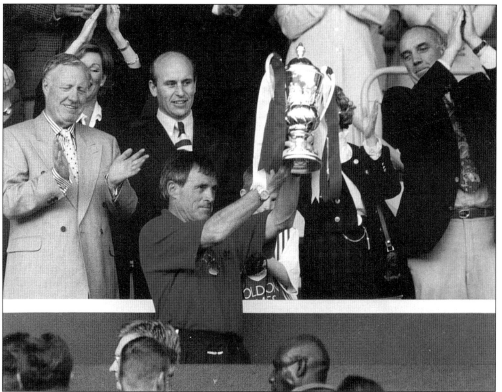

A moment of pride and joy for manager Dario Gradi as he holds the play-off trophy aloft.

Following the medal presentations, it is out on the pitch for the traditional photograph. The placard says it all – Crewe Alexandra are the play-off winners.

Shaun Smith, Crewe's long-serving captain, gives the photographers a chance to capture his delight.

Leaving the pitch at Gresty Road after the England Under-18 side have defeated Russia 3-2 on 5 February 1998. Seth Johnson scored the winning goal for England, a double delight as it was in front of Crewe fans.

Crewe record their first victory in Division One when they visit Carrow Road in August 1997.

Almost there – Colin Little scores after 22 minutes at The Hawthorns. This goal proved sufficient to clinch another victory.

The Stadium of Light, the new home of Sunderland, saw Crewe playing in front of 40,441 spectators. Kevin Street and Gareth Whalley warm to the task in an exciting game.

An achievement for the club was gaining League doubles over their Potteries rivals. *Top*: action from the game against Stoke at the Britannia Stadium in December 1997. *Bottom*: Mark Foran celebrates his goal at Vale Park in January 1998.

Tuesday 3 March 1998 was the day that Crewe Alexandra's manager, Dario Gradi, received the MBE at Buckingham Palace for his services to football.